Writing Skills
Teacher's Book

Writing Skills

A problem-solving approach
for upper-intermediate and
more advanced students

Teacher's Book

Norman Coe and Robin Rycroft

CAMBRIDGE
UNIVERSITY PRESS

PUBLISHED BY THE PRESS SYNDICATE OF THE UNIVERSITY OF CAMBRIDGE
The Pitt Building, Trumpington Street, Cambridge, United Kingdom

CAMBRIDGE UNIVERSITY PRESS
The Edinburgh Building, Cambridge CB2 2RU, UK
40 West 20th Street, New York, NY 10011–4211, USA
10 Stamford Road, Oakleigh, VIC 3166, Australia
Ruiz de Alarcón 13, 28014 Madrid, Spain
Dock House, The Waterfront, Cape Town 8001, South Africa

http://www.cambridge.org

First published 1983
Tenth printing 2001

Printed in the United Kingdom at the University Press, Cambridge

A catalogue record for this book is available from the British Library

ISBN 0 521 28143 1 Teacher's Book
ISBN 0 521 28142 3 Student's Book

For Nellie Coe, who helped in a dark hour.

Contents

Introduction

AIMS

Writing Skills aims to help foreign learners of English to improve their
writing of letters, stories, and other texts. Speaking is usually a spontaneous
activity, but writing is a deliberate, conscious process, which can and
should be planned and organised. The various exercises in *Writing Skills* are
designed to make learners aware of what a well-written text is, and how it
is different from a series of poorly connected sentences. Having become
conscious of the differences, the learners then have the opportunity to
practise the skills that are needed in order to write well.

Teachers should note that *Writing Skills* concentrates on the skills that
are specific to the *writing* of English. There are other aspects of language,
such as vocabulary and grammar, that are common to all uses of language.
These aspects are important to writing, of course, but they are not *specific*
to writing. Although the activities in this book will clearly provide students
with practice in vocabulary and grammar, this is not the main aim of the
material.

LEVEL AND PROGRESSION

Writing Skills is for learners who have studied about 400–500 hours of
English and are approaching the level of the Cambridge First Certificate in
English examination. The skills practised here will be useful as preparation
for this examination, as well as for other examinations where writing is
important.

Writing Skills is a source book, not a course book. In other words, the
material does not progress in difficulty from Unit 1 through to Unit 9, and
learners do not need to have done the earlier exercises before doing the later
ones. Rather the book provides learners and their teachers with material
that can be exploited to suit their particular needs. For example, if punctuation is a particularly weak point for a group of learners, then they can work
through all the exercises on punctuation without doing the other exercises
in the various units.

LEARNERS' PROBLEMS IN WRITING

Here are some of the main reasons why a learner's writing may be difficult to understand or defective in some other way:

a) The sentences may not have clear punctuation: there may be commas and full stops without any good reason, or there may be no punctuation where there should be some. This is dealt with mainly in the **Punctuation** exercises (see page 5).

b) The ideas may not have been presented in an order that easily makes sense to the reader. This is treated in the exercises on **Scrambled sentences** (see page 6) and also in the **Selection and ordering** exercises (see page 11).

c) The relation between the ideas may not be clear because of the absence, or inappropriate use, of linking words and phrases, such as *although, for example, lastly, on the other hand,* and so on. This question is covered in the exercises on **Linking words** (see page 8).

d) The writer's attitude to what he or she is writing may not be clear: is he or she describing, suggesting or criticising something? This problem is taken up in the exercises on **Attitude words** (see page 8), and also to some extent in the exercises on **Reporting words** (see page 9).

e) The ideas may not be grouped together into distinct paragraphs, or the learner may begin practically every sentence on a new line. Again, a paragraph – or a longer text – may not begin with an introduction that starts the reader in the right direction; similarly, the paragraph – or text – may not end appropriately. All of these problems are dealt with in the exercises on **Paragraphs** (see page 10).

f) A text may contain ideas that are not really relevant to what the writer wants to express, or the writer may find it difficult to think of enough ideas. This is considered in the exercises on **Selection and ordering** (see page 11).

While it is useful to work on all these different aspects of writing in distinct exercises, it is also important that learners should have practice in combining the separate skills in one complete, well-written text. Opportunities for this will be found in the exercises on **Text comparison** (see page 12), **Text based on a conversation** (see page 13), and **Text based on visual information** (see page 13). In addition there are suggestions for further writing activities given in **Ideas for further practice** at the end of each unit.

APPROACH

In a word our approach is: learning by doing. There are various reasons for this. First, learners generally find that doing something (i.e. being relatively active) is more interesting than being told about it (i.e. being relatively passive.) Second, if learners come to understand through using their own resources to solve problems, then their understanding will probably be more thorough, and they are more likely to retain what they have learnt. Third, it is only when learners put something into practice that any incorrect or imperfect learning is revealed, and it is revealed both to the learners themselves and to the teacher. Our experience is, then, that learning by doing is more interesting and more efficient.

Teachers should note that in some cases the stated purpose of an activity is not its only purpose. For instance, the stated aim of the **Scrambled sentences** exercises is to work out the original order of the sentences. However, in order to carry this out, the learners will have to concentrate on the meaning and function of devices that join sentences into texts. In this case, the process is in fact a more important aim than the product.

GROUP WORK

Closely connected with our approach is our belief in group work. Our instructions for each exercise invariably propose that the task, or at least the first part of it, should be attempted by a number of learners working together in a group. This is because a group of learners will – between them – usually have the knowledge and the skills needed to do the exercises.

It is also worth noting that an individual learner's ability to organise his ideas in writing is often independent of his general language level. Some otherwise successful language learners may have a poor sense of organisation, and vice versa. However, when several learners work in a group and pool their abilities, then together they will normally be able to contribute all the elements necessary to produce clear writing. This pooling of abilities, and the discussion that arises during the exercise, will gradually strengthen every individual's skill in writing English.

We would like to point out that group work does not normally end with the students being given the right answer by the teacher. The process of arguing your way to the right answer can be continued even after the small group task is completed. One such way is for someone to write the various suggestions on the board, and the class can then discuss the differences, (see **Scrambled sentences: How**, page 6). A second way is to join each group with one or two others, making a smaller number of larger groups, and these larger groups can simultaneously discuss the different solutions represented in the group, (see **Linking words/Attitude words: How**, page 8). A third possibility is to split up the original groups and form others of the same size. For example, if there were four original groups:
A B C   D E F   G H I J   K L M,
then the new groups could be:
A G L   B D H M   C E I   F J K.
Incidentally, the teacher does not need to organise this in detail. The instructions need simply be: 'Get into new groups of three or four in a way that no one else in your new group is from your old group.' With a bit of practice – and shuffling of chairs – the learners will do the rest.

TYPES OF EXERCISES

UNITS

	Punctuation	Scrambled sentences	Linking words	Attitude words	Reporting words	Paragraphs	Selection and ordering	Text comparison	Text based on a conversation	Text based on visual information	Other	Ideas for further practice
1. Informal letters	1.1	1.2	1.3	1.4	1.5	1.6	-	1.7	1.8	1.9	-	1.10
2. Formal letters I	2.1	2.2	2.3	2.4	-	2.5	2.6	2.7	-	2.8	-	2.9
3. Formal letters II	3.1	3.2	3.3	3.4	3.5	3.6	3.7	3.8	-	3.9	3.10	3.11
4. Reports	4.1	4.2	4.3	-	-	4.4	4.5	4.6	4.7	4.8	-	4.9
5. Brochures and guides	5.1	5.2	5.3	-	-	5.4	5.5	5.6	-	5.7	-	5.8
6. Articles	6.1	6.2	6.3	-	-	6.4	6.5	-	6.6	6.7	6.8	6.9
7. Instructions	7.1	7.2	-	-	7.3	7.4	-	7.5	-	7.6	-	7.7
8. Stories	8.1	8.2	8.3	-	8.4	8.5	-	8.6	8.7	8.8	-	8.9
9. Business correspondence	9.1	9.2	9.3	-	9.4	9.5	-	9.6	-	9.7	-	9.8

Types of exercise

Every unit contains a wide variety of exercises and activities, but there is no fixed pattern running through all the units. Instead of allowing a rigid framework to dictate the final shape of the units, we have taken a more pragmatic line. In the first place, the exercises that we originally wrote to a large extent grew naturally out of the unit theme (Letters, Reports, etc.). Those original exercises were then tried out at many schools in several different countries. The feedback from these trials allowed us to improve or reject unsatisfactory exercises, and we have kept a range of the best exercises for each unit, though not the same range for all of them.

The nine units contain from seven to eleven different exercises, as can be seen from the chart on the opposite page. In discussing the different types of exercise below, we have provided the following:

Under the heading **What** there is a description of what each exercise type consists of.

Under the heading **How** there are suggestions as to how each type of exercise can be approached in the classroom.

Under the heading **Why** we explain the reason for each exercise-type within the overall objective of learning to write better.

Under the heading **Which** we list all the exercises of each type that are to be found throughout the material.

PUNCTUATION

What   The punctuation exercises cover uses of all the main punctuation marks (full stops, commas, and so on), as well as capital letters and apostrophes.

5

How In groups of two or three, learners first study given models which in many cases are contrasted with incorrect forms or forms that have different meanings. These models are followed by examples where the learners – sometimes in groups, sometimes working individually – have to use the punctuation marks in question.

Why Badly punctuated writing is usually difficult to understand, as well as giving a slovenly impression. In English many uses of punctuation give a clear indication of the sense of the passage, and so learners should be encouraged to use it properly.

Which There are nine exercises of this type:
1.1 Capital letters
2.1 Apostrophes
3.1 Commas in non-defining relative clauses, contrasted with defining relative clauses
4.1 Places where punctuation is not used
5.1 Full stops, semicolons and commas
6.1 Colons and semicolons
7.1 Commas and full stops in extended writing
8.1 Inverted commas for speech
9.1 Mixed punctuation

SCRAMBLED SENTENCES

What A text has been separated into its component sentences; these appear in the exercise in random order. Learners must try to recompose the text, i.e. they must decide on the correct order of the sentences. Certain words and phrases have been underlined or printed in bold type to draw attention to the part they play in joining the original text together. (Words and phrases that join sentences into texts are sometimes called 'textual devices'.)

These exercises are relatively easy, but they are interesting, and they give the learners a good general idea of what makes a text different from an unconnected string of sentences.

How It is a great help to photocopy the text, making one copy for each group. The copies should be cut into strips, each strip having one sentence. (This makes it easy to make different arrangements and to read them.) Working in groups of two or three, the learners should read the texts, paying particular attention to the words and phrases underlined. Each group then works out the best order through discussion. When the groups have reached a conclusion, their suggested orders should be compared. The teacher, or one of the learners, can (without comment at this point) write the orders suggested by the various groups on the board, producing columns that can then be compared, for example:

Group	1	2	3	4	5
	d	d	d	d	d
	f	f	f	f	f
	e	b	b	e	b
	j	e	h	j	e
	b	j	e	b	j
	h	h	j	h	h
	g	c	c	c	c
	c	i	i	i	i
	i	a	a	a	a
	a	g	g	g	g

(The correct answer, let us suppose, is that reached by groups 2 and 5.) The teacher can mark the sequences that all the groups have in common and which are in fact correct like this:

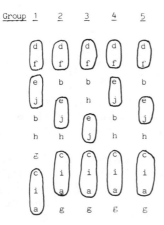

The teacher can now ask the learners to give their reasons for and against those sequences where there are differences. If necessary, the teacher can point out what it is in the text that gives the clue to the right order, which often means referring again to the words underlined. On the whole the learners should argue their way to the correct solution rather than simply be told what it is.

Why As with many classroom activities, the stated aim of the exercise, i.e. to find the right order of the sentences, is not its only purpose. As well as providing an opportunity for group work and for class discussion, this kind of exercise helps learners to see for themselves the importance of the 'textual devices', (though this term, of course, need not be used.) Moreover, by discussing the various differences, the learners will gradually find out exactly how these textual devices operate. For this reason the discussion should not be passed over by the teacher simply telling the learners what the right answer is.

Which   There are nine exercises of this type:
1.2, 2.2, 3.2, 4.2, 5.2, 6.2, 7.2, 8.2 and 9.2.

LINKING WORDS AND ATTITUDE WORDS

For our purposes we define a *linking word* as a word or phrase which shows the logical relation between sentences or between clauses. For example:

The most important oil-exporting countries, **such as** Saudi Arabia, Kuwait and Iraq, are concentrated in a small geographical area, **namely** the Middle East. There are, **however,** several other important exporters of crude oil in other parts of the world.

Here the words in bold type are linking words.

An *attitude word*, on the other hand, is a word or phrase that shows the writer's attitude to what he is writing. For example:

Obviously, if the scandal became public knowledge, some officials would have to resign, and **personally,** I don't think that would be such a bad thing.

Here the words in bold type are attitude words.

What   The linking or attitude words have been removed from a text and learners must supply a suitable word to fill the blank, either by choosing from a given list or thinking of a word themselves.

How   Working in groups of two or three, learners should try to complete the exercise, deciding which is the most appropriate word or phrase. When each group has finished, the conclusions (and differences) can be discussed by the whole class, using a procedure similar to the one described in *Scrambled sentences: How,* page 6. Alternatively, each group can join with one or two other groups, and these larger groups can compare their answers. When these two phases are completed, the remaining problems can be taken up for discussion in the whole class.

Why   While we realise — here and elsewhere — that it is not easy for teachers to resist the temptation to 'give the right answer and get on with it', we would insist that the discussion about the right answer is a very important part of the learning process. During the discussion the learners are concentrating on the reasons why a word is appropriate in a particular context, and this is exactly what we want them to be thinking about. Obviously it matters which word is chosen, but it is just as important that learners become aware that there are good and bad reasons for their choices. In using exercises of this type, it is our experience that there is a positive transfer when learners are set freer writing tasks.

Which   There are eight *Linking words* exercises:
1.3, 2.3, 3.3, 4.3, 5.3, 6.3, 8.3 and 9.3.
There are three *Attitude words* exercises:
1.4, 2.4 and 3.4.

REPORTING WORDS

What   Learners first compare two reported speech versions of something given as direct speech. In each case, one is a strictly mechanical conversion, and the other is more realistic. Learners then have to report other examples of direct speech, choosing from a given list of reporting words. Finally, learners have to produce their own examples to illustrate the use of certain reporting words.

How   As usual, learners share their ideas and knowledge in solving the initial problem and producing suitable sentences. Discussion as to why such and such an alternative was chosen is again an essential part of the exercise. The initial group work leads on to individual application.

Why   In each case, the two given models are — in some sense — both correct, and this will often lead to a discussion that is more wide-ranging than simply which is the more suitable. The fact is that — with the lamentable exception of some classroom exercises and some exams — the reporting of speech is never an automatic application of strict rules (e.g. present tenses become past tenses, and so on). Rather the reporter, taking into account various aspects of the situation, chooses a reporting word to give the feeling of the message and his attitude towards it, e.g. *demand, suggest, warn, urge*. Obviously, different reporters will choose different ways of reporting the same speech. For example, a suspect says to a policeman: 'I'm innocent.' Later the suspect might report: 'I insisted that I was innocent', while the policeman might choose to say: 'He claimed he was innocent.'

Consequently textbooks cannot use mechanical exercises to help learners to use reporting words and reported speech properly. The exercises in this book are designed to:

a)   broaden the range of reporting words that learners use (i.e. not simply *say, tell* and *ask* every time), and

b)   make learners aware that the reporting of speech is not an automatic process, but rather they should think about the circumstances of each case and choose a reporting word accordingly.

Which   There are five exercises of this type:
1.5, 3.5, 7.3, 8.4 and 9.4.

PARAGRAPHS

What We have tried to show that well-written paragraphs make a written text easier to understand. Each paragraph should have a first sentence that introduces the rest of the paragraph, and a final sentence that summarises or properly concludes it. At the level of an extended text (say, a letter) the first paragraph should outline the main points of the letter, and the last paragraph should round it off.

As in the case of *Linking words* and *Attitude words*, these exercises are of various types, including:
a) choosing the most appropriate answer from a list,
b) making up a suitable answer to fill a blank, and
c) writing the rest of the text, given a leading sentence or paragraph.

How Again learners should work in groups, one member of each group acting as secretary; the findings of the groups should be discussed. It is essential, of course, that the sentence or paragraph that has been chosen or written should be appropriate to the rest of the text in both content and style. In discussing the suggestions, it is important that learners should again express their reasons for their preferences so that all the learners gradually become more aware of what makes one possibility preferable to another. A similar procedure to that suggested in *Scrambled sentences: How*, page 6, or in *Linking words and attitude words: How*, page 8, could be adopted to allow groups to compare their answers.

Why In general, if a text is divided into well-written paragraphs, it will be easier to read. More particularly, rapid and efficient reading is only possible if the text has been written to allow for this. It should be possible for a reader to skim through a long passage by reading the first paragraph, then the first sentence of each successive paragraph, and the final paragraph. This should give the reader an overall idea of what the text contains, so it is important to use first sentences to introduce the topic, and it is preferable to use final sentences to sum up. Our various exercises on *Paragraphs* aim to show learners how this can be done.

Note: We accept, of course, that there are more ways of organising paragraphs and passages than the one used here. However, as with vocabulary and grammar, the native user of the language can allow himself a wider range and greater latitude in his choice of expression; the foreign learner, on the other hand, needs to achieve mastery of a smaller, but generally serviceable, range of possibilities.

Which There are nine exercises on paragraphs:
1.6, 2.5, 3.6, 4.4, 5.4, 6.4, 7.4, 8.5 and 9.5.

SELECTION AND ORDERING

What
These exercises give instructions for a written text — a letter, an article, and so on — together with a long list of ideas for possible inclusion. Working in groups, learners choose the most relevant ideas from the list and reject the others. When each group has made its selection, the next step is to group the ideas so as to provide the contents for a number of paragraphs, each one dealing with one aspect of the subject. Groups must also decide on the best order for the paragraphs. Finally, learners should exploit this preparation in writing the complete text.

How
Each member of the group should first read through the list silently, making a note of the ideas he or she would include.
Then the group should work through the list, marking off all the ideas where everyone agrees, and noting those ideas where there is disagreement. The disputed ideas should be discussed and, although the time allowed for this may be limited, the discussion should not be passed over.

At the stage of grouping sentences into paragraphs, the task can again be first attempted individually and silently, and later the group can compare their suggestions. At the end of the planning, and before the learners write the final text, groups can exchange their conclusions for the sake of comparison. But there is no reason to insist that all the plans must be rigidly the same.

In two cases there is an opportunity for practising a preliminary stage: the groups have to make up their own lists of ideas. The groups should be given a fixed time to produce as long a list as possible. It is important at this stage that *all* ideas are noted down; a group secretary should make notes, and there should be a minimum of discussion. Now, starting from the lists that they themselves have generated, groups can go through the steps outlined above. (Although only two exercises have been provided with this added opportunity, other topics — chosen by the learners or by the teacher — could well be treated in the same way.)

Note: Working through every step of either version of this exercise will take a great deal of class time. Although the time would probably be well spent, teachers might choose to limit the class time devoted to this either by restricting the task to one or two of the steps, or by setting some of the steps for homework. For instance, for one homework learners could read through the items and make a preliminary choice. In the subsequent lesson they could work in groups up to the point of planning the final passage. Then, again for homework, each learner could write his or her version based on this preparation.

Why
First, let us look at the task based on a given list. What one person considers relevant, another may consider irrelevant; again, the same fact may be relevant in one circumstance, but not in another. These exercises are designed to make learners aware of what

makes something relevant by forcing them to consider not only *what* they are writing, but also *why* they are writing and *to whom*. Let us emphasise that there is no one indisputable answer in all cases. Although some items in the lists will be quickly accepted or rejected by everybody, others will lead to disagreement. It is most important that these items should be discussed, so that arguments can be produced and evaluated. It is only when people are forced to defend their view that they will realise the implications of what relevance is.

Now let us turn to the reasons for asking learners to generate their own lists. In the first place, it is an enjoyable activity, for learners are seldom allowed the freedom to say anything that comes into their heads. But further, it is essential that the creative element in writing should be stimulated. In our experience, where learners are not given opportunities like this, they often complain that they can't write compositions because they haven't got anything to say. This kind of exercise is designed to train learners to open their minds in order to generate enough material for possible inclusion in their writing.

The two versions of this exercise show the learners that there is a difference between having an idea and choosing to use it. If learners can learn to generate a lot of ideas, and also learn to discriminate relevant ideas from less relevant ones, then they will have a solid base for anything that they decide to write.

Which There are five exercises of this type:
2.6, 3.7, 4.5, 5.5 and 6.5.

TEXT COMPARISON

What Two passages have been written on the same subject. One of them is badly written, and the other is well written. Learners must read the two passages, and decide which one they prefer, and why. Learners are then asked either to rewrite the passage they did not like, or to write a third passage based on additional information.

Teachers should note that there are no mistakes of vocabulary or grammar (sentence structure) in any of the passages; the faults are textual ones.

How Working in groups of two or three, learners should first read the two passages silently, and then compare their views with each other. They should ask themselves (a) which of the two is easier to follow, and (b) what are the specific differences that make one preferable to the other. One member of the group should act as secretary, making a list of the features mentioned by the group. After a suitable time, each group should make a brief report to the rest of the class. As we have suggested with other exercises, time should be allowed for any differences of opinion to be resolved. The teacher should try to limit his or her contributions to asking questions rather than to giving answers.

After the discussion, learners should complete the second part of the task, i.e. writing or rewriting. If time is not available for this in class, it could be done for homework. Where possible, learners should later compare their versions with each other.

Why At the level of a complete text, learners can best appreciate the differences between a well-written text and a badly connected set of sentences by seeing the differences for themselves. Once they have found out why one text is easier to read and to understand than another, then they will be able to apply this knowledge in their own writing. We have found that learners who have had this practice become more critical of the shortcomings in their own writing, and are better able to put things right.

Which There are eight exercises of this type:
1.7, 2.7, 3.8, 4.6, 5.6, 7.5, 8.6 and 9.6.

TEXT BASED ON A CONVERSATION OR ON VISUAL INFORMATION

What In these exercises learners are provided with, in the first type, a conversation, and, in the second type, visual information, e.g. a diagram, a map or photographs. In most cases there is also a model text on a related subject; in earlier units the guidance provided by the model tends to be greater than in the later units.

How Learners first read silently through the given material; then, in groups, they discuss which aspects of this material can usefully be exploited in carrying out the set task. This final writing task will be individual, so all group members should make notes at this point. Groups can then compare their ideas (in ways that we have suggested for other exercise types) before learners tackle the writing itself, which can be done either in class or at home.

Why These exercises are included as a way of integrating all the separate skills that the other exercises treat individually. We have placed these exercises towards the end of the units because they are more demanding than the ones that practise specific skills. However, learners do not need to have done the earlier exercises in order to tackle these.

Which There are four *Texts based on a conversation:*
1.8, 4.7, 6.6 and 8.7.
There are nine *Texts based on visual information:*
1.9, 2.8, 3.9, 4.8, 5.7, 6.7, 7.6, 8.8 and 9.7.

OTHER TYPES OF EXERCISE

We have included two exercises which do not fit into any of the above categories; for these we refer you to the exercises themselves: 3.10 and 6.8.

There are also *Ideas for further practice* at the end of each unit.

Key to exercises

This key contains answers to all the objective exercises in the Student's Book. Model answers are also provided when the exercise requires students to write a text incorporating given information. When both form and content is left to the student, no model is provided.

1 INFORMAL LETTERS

1.1

8 Was Professor Blunt working for the Queen of England?
9 The British Prime Minister met the German Foreign Minister for talks.
10 Is Lake Geneva near Mont Blanc?
11 On Thursday we're going to the Museum of Natural History.
12 The suggestion was made by Captain Jones on behalf of General Taylor.
13 Is Dr Spock American or Canadian?
14 Last year Good Friday was on April 1st.

1.2

h j e l b n c m f k a g i d

1.3

1 (b)   2 (a)   3 (c)   4 (b)   5 (a)   6 (c)   7 (a)
8 (a)   9 (c)   10 (a)   11 (b)   12 (b)   13 (a)   14 (b)
15 Besides *or* What's more
16 because
17 such as *or* for instance
18 In other words
19 may
20 even
21 However
22 For instance

1.4

1 (a)   2 (b)   3 (b)   4 (c)   5 (a)   6 (c)   7 (b)
8 (a)   9 (c)   10 (a)

1.5

In a way both (a) and (b) are correct; however, (b) follows the so-called rules for reported speech slavishly, while (a) provides a more concise report. It is the reporting word *blame* that makes this possible, since reporting words express the main feeling of what was said, allowing the report itself to be kept short. In real life, therefore, (a) will virtually always be preferred to (b).

1 Angela explained (to me) how to get to the post office.
2 Mrs Jones advised Dick to write (to them) at once and explain what had happened.
3 Sara called Brian a fool.
4 Penny suggested going by train.
  Penny suggested that they should go by train.
5 The young lady insisted that somebody should pay for the broken window.

1.7

The second letter is to be preferred because the first consists of many short, unconnected sentences. One improved version of the first letter is:

Dear Aunt Nellie,

I've just started work, and I'd like to tell you about my experiences so far. I'm working as a typist in an insurance office which has about forty other people. Most of the time I type letters for a very kind man called Mr Merriam, who is manager of the Claims Department. He gives me my work, and I take it back to him when I've typed it.

There are all kinds of different people in the office: some rude, some noisy, some funny. I've made friends with another typist called Susan; her boss is a Mrs Jones, who is manager of the Accounts Department. Susan and I get on very well together, and we go to a nice little cafe for lunch, which costs about a pound.

You know that I've been trained as a typist, so the work here is easy for me. The office is very clean and modern, though I find the atmosphere strange and a bit difficult to get used to. Transport from home to work is no problem for me: I first catch a 26 bus, change at Bidlam Square, and then continue on a number 12. It takes about 20 minutes.

1.8

One possible version of the letter is:

Dear Mother and Father,

I'm just writing to let you know that we're all well, and I hope you are, too. Unfortunately, I've got some rather bad news for you: I'm afraid I've had an accident. It's nothing to worry about, and I'm perfectly all right, but I'm afraid I made a bit of a mess of Jeff's car. Anyway, here's what happened.

We were on our way to Carol's after a long party, and I suppose it must have been about eleven o'clock. You know she lives out in the middle of nowhere. Well, the last few miles are really dark and deserted. I now realise I was probably going a bit too fast for a country lane because, although the road was fairly straight, I drove up onto the kerb and went into a tree.

Of course, Jeff was absolutely furious, and started shouting at me and cursing. After we'd argued for a few moments, we decided to look at the damage, and he calmed down a bit. Well, we found we could move the car, but the wing was catching on the wheel, so we couldn't drive it. I tried to pull the wing clear, but I didn't manage it.

Anyway, Jeff went off to phone for a breakdown lorry, but while he was away, I had another go at the wing and this time succeeded in pulling it right off. I threw it onto the back seat, and by the time Jeff got back we were ready to go – so we didn't need the breakdown lorry at all. Jeff has more or less forgiven me now, but he was very angry with me for a few days. I suppose I was a bit careless.

Well, that's all for now. Next time I write I hope I'll have better news for you.

1.9

Possible versions of the two letters are:

... then you come to a long, almost straight road with a golf course on the right, and some woods on the left a little further on. On your right you'll now see Clatterbridge Hospital, which is enormous, like a miniature city. At the junction immediately after the hospital turn right, and carry on until you see a rugby field on the left. This is where you should slow down because you have to take the next turning on the right, just before the petrol station. Our house is just up this road on the right.

I hope you can follow all this. Anyway, we're all looking forward to seeing you very much.

Dear Laura,

I'm very happy to hear that you'll be coming to Chacklow Hall for our New Year's Eve party. You may have some difficulty in getting here from Raby, so I'll describe the route for you.

Go past the rugby field to the main road, and turn right there. Follow the road round to the hospital, and turn left immediately after it. The road bends round to the left and then is almost straight past the golf course and the old beacon, both on the left. Keep going as straight as you can, and you'll cross over the railway just before you come to a T-junction, where you have to turn left. You'll see the university buildings on the right, and at the next crossroads turn left. Chacklow Hall is just along this road on the right. You can't miss it.

Have a happy Christmas, and see you at the party!

2 FORMAL LETTERS I

2.1

1 I think it's an elephant, but it's so far away I can't see its trunk.
2 John's brother's wife went to the grocer's for us.
3 The women's changing room is opposite the men's.
4 The Smiths provided the food and the Jacksons organised the transport.
5 Two wrongs don't make a right.
6 This car can't be my parents' because theirs is quite old.
7 Peter asked Jenny's father for all the customers' addresses.
8 The girls' entrance used to be separate from the boys'; now there's only one entrance for everybody.
9 She won't go to the dentist's because it's too late.
10 What's the sense in saying it's Jack's?
11 My skis are new; hers are my mother's old ones.
12 Its exact translation is somewhat difficult, isn't it?

2.2

f   c   k   h   h   b   i   d   l   a   j   e   g
Paragraphs: f   ckhbi   dlaje   g
Some people would make the first paragraph: fckhbi.

2.3

1 (a), (b) or (c)
2 (a), (b) or (d)
3 (a), (b) or (d)
4 (a)
5 (a) or (c)
6 (b) or (c)
7 (b) or (d)
8 (b) or (d)
9 (a), (b) or (c)
10 (a)

2.4

1 (c)	2 (c)	3 (c)	4 (a)	5 (b)	6 (a)	7 (b)
8 (b)	9 (b)	10 (b)				

2.5

Preferred first sentence: (d).
Preferred last sentence: (b).

2.7

The first letter is to be preferred because here the points are collected into paragraphs, each paragraph dealing with a different aspect of the matter. The divisions (not really paragraphs) of the second letter are pointless; it only makes sense to divide a text into paragraphs if each of these treats a different aspect of the subject.

One possible version of Juan Gomez' letter is:

Dear Sirs,

I am writing to apply for a British Council scholarship to study in Britain. I did my five years' basic training in medicine at Salamanca University. After this I successfully completed a one-year postgraduate course in Ophthalmology at the Barcelona General Hospital, where I am at present serving a two-year probation in the Eye Clinic.

As a result of the publication in 1976 of my article in The Lancet entitled 'Soft and Rigid Contact Lenses', which was based on a survey of 37 patients over 6 months, I made contact with Dr Jermyn of St Thomas's Hospital and with Dr Askerholm of the University College Hospital. I have received their help and advice with my current research project, which is a two-year survey of the acceptance of various types of contact lenses in 200 patients.

Despite their help, I feel that I cannot make real progress in this field unless I can actually have day-to-day contact with these specialists. I would therefore like to continue my research at either St Thomas's or UCH as soon as my probationary period here is completed, and I would like to study in Britain for two years.

I enclose a detailed curriculum vitae and an offprint of my article, together with a letter of recommendation from Dr Jermyn.

---

3 FORMAL LETTERS II

3.1

In English there are two main kinds of relative clause. One kind defines the part of the sentence to which it refers; these defining relative clauses cannot be used with a noun phrase that is already definite. Defining relative clauses have no commas. The other kind provides additional information about something that is already defined; these non-defining relative clauses must be separated by commas from the rest of the sentence. (If a non-defining clause ends the sentence, the second comma is replaced by a full stop; see for example 5b.)

1　Only (b) is correct, because **Everest** is a definite description.

2　Only (a) is correct. **The river** is defined by **that runs through Paris** and **The river that runs through Paris** is the subject of the sentence. A subject can never be separated from its verb by a comma, (although, of course, a non-defining relative clause *with a comma at each end* can come between a subject and its verb; see for example 6(b).)

3　In (a) **who is in the merchant navy** defines which cousin we are talking about; in other words, this implies that there are several cousins under discussion. In (b) **who is in the merchant navy** merely gives extra information; in other words, there is only one cousin under discussion here.

4　With an indefinite expression like **someone** the only point of adding a relative clause is in order to define it. Thus only (a) makes sense.

5　In (b) it is assumed that the addressee will know which letter is being referred to without any further definition; **which arrived today** is, in other words, additional information. It would be unusual for someone to write thanking for one of a number of possible letters, namely the one that arrived today. Thus (a) is extremely improbable.

6　(b) is correct; (a) is not. Compare 1.

7　(a) implies that there were several windows; (b) implies that there was only one. Compare 3.

8　(b) is correct; (a) is not. Compare 1.

9　(b) is correct; (a) is not. The only use of **which would suit you best** would be to define which dates were being discussed.

10　(a) implies that some girls (i.e. those who worked hard) got a bonus, but the others did not. (b) implies that all the girls (perhaps in contrast with the boys or the women) were given a bonus.

11　Compare 6.　　16　Compare 3.
12　Compare 5.　　17　Compare 10.
13　Compare 9.　　18　Compare 4.
14　Compare 1.　　19　Compare 8.
15　Compare 10.　　20　Compare 3.

3.2

f d j h b e i a g c

3.3

1 (b)	2 (b)	3 (c)	4 (a)	5 (a)	6 (c)	7 (c)
8 (a)	9 (b)	10 (d)	11 (c)	12 (b)	13 (d)	
14 (b)	15 (d)					

16 In spite of that
17 therefore, (consequently, for this reason)
18 If not
19 namely
20 After all
21 What is more, (Besides, Moreover)
22 As a result, (Consequently, For this reason, This is why)
23 even

3.4

1 (a)	2 (a)	3 (c)	4 (b)	5 (b)	6 (c)	7 (a)
8 (b)	9 (a)	10 (c)				

3.5

In a way both (a) and (b) are correct; however, (a) follows the so-called rules for reported speech slavishly, while (b) provides a more concise report. It is the reporting word *claim* that makes this possible, since reporting words express the main feeling of what was said, allowing the report itself to be kept short. In real life (b) will virtually always be preferred to (a).

1 Jim wondered what would happen if he refused.
2 The Council refused to treat our (their) case as important.
3 Sheila's boyfriend accused her of going out with other men behind his back.
4 Fred denied being responsible for the fire.
   Fred denied that he was responsible for the fire.
5 The official announced that the flight would leave at about 3 o'clock.

3.6

Preferred first sentence: (e)
Preferred last sentence: (c)
Possible first and last sentences for the second part are:

I am writing to express my concern at the large number of so-called 'amusement arcades' which have suddenly appeared in Loucester.

In conclusion, may I say that I feel it is our duty as parents to educate our children to amuse themselves in a healthy and constructive way, and also provide the facilities for them to do so.

3.8

The first letter is to be preferred; the second letter contains many personal pronouns that are not clearly related to a previous noun phrase. A better version of the second letter is:

Dear Sir,

Last Saturday some friends of mine and I were spending a pleasant afternoon playing bridge on the balcony of our house, when some employees of the Merseyside Water Board started making a terrible noise in the road outside. When I went down and asked the foreman what was happening, he told me that the company was digging up a section of the road to do some repairs on the water main. The foreman said that he understood my complaint, and that he would pass it on to the company.

I fully realise that the water company cannot send workers only at times which suit me, but in my opinion Saturday seems to be the wrong day to choose. Must the citizens of Merseyside always accept what these **public** companies decide?

3.9

A possible letter to accompany the second diagram is:

Dear Sirs,

I enclose my entry for the Linton Gazette SRC design competition. The idea that lies behind much of what I have included is my belief that sport should not be separated from other aspects of our daily lives, and that people playing sport should not need to be separated from their families. This conviction has influenced my design in a number of ways.

First, it explains the existence of the restaurant, the small theatre and the meeting rooms. For one thing, these facilities would give sportsmen and women the chance to combine sport with other activities, and again, these rooms might attract visitors who are not particularly interested in sport.

Second, it is the thinking behind the unusual transport facilities. People play sports to keep healthy, and I feel that everybody

---

➤➤→

should be encouraged to take care of their health even outside the
centre. I have therefore kept car parking to a minimum while
providing extensive space for bicycles. This, I hope, will
persuade people to leave their cars at home and instead cycle
to the centre. I would also like to arrange for a special bus
that runs direct from the bus station to the centre.

The third point is that there is a provision for all the family
within the centre. Instead of only one or two members of the
family attending the centre, with my design everybody can come.
There is a nursery for the very young and a playground for older
children; and retired people will be able to sit in the gardens
or around the playground watching the children at play.

In conclusion, I would like to say that I have included something
for almost all sporting tastes; the one major thing that I have
not included is a full-size sports pitch (for football, hockey,
etc.) because there are already several of these in Linton.
I hope the judges will find my design original and interesting.

4 REPORTS

4.1

13, 14, 15 need no punctuation.
16 Jenny said that the work was very difficult. 'It's not really difficult,' I
said, 'but it is time-consuming.' 17, 18, 19, 20 need no punctuation.
21 My sister is that girl reading the newspaper, and the one next to her is
my cousin.
22 They wrote to us to find out what had caused the delay, but we couldn't
tell them anything.
(In 21 and 22 it would be possible to omit the comma, but it is normal
to put one before coordinating conjunctions when the two clauses are
long, as here.)
23 They wanted to know whether I could start at once. 'Not at once,' I
replied, 'but perhaps by tomorrow afternoon.'
24 Needs no punctuation.

4.2

g c i f b h e a j d

4.3

| 1 (c) | 2 (a) | 3 (c) | 4 (c) | 5 (c) | 6 (c) | 7 (c) |

8 (c)   9 (c)   10 (d)

11 At the beginning
12 At first
13 in the end
14 At last
15 first, firstly
16 last, lastly
17 at the end

Learners should come to a realisation that there are really three different groups of phrases here, each with its own function:
1 **At first, in the beginning, at last, in the end.**
   These are used to indicate points in the chronological development of a story; a typical development would be: at first ....; later ....; and/but in the end. Note that **at last** (but not **in the end**) can be used as an exclamation at the appearance of a long-awaited climax.
2 **First, second, third,** etc., **last;** or **firstly, secondly, thirdly,** etc., **lastly.**
   These are used to indicate separate points in a list; in technical and scientific writing we often use (a), (b), (c) etc., or 1, 2, 3, etc., for the same purpose.
3 **At the beginning; at the end.**
   These must always have — explicitly or implicitly — a prepositional phrase with **of**: at the beginning of the story/film/book/match, etc.; at the end of the play/presentation/book/novel, etc.

4.4

Paragraph (a) introduces the main argument of the report, but it is in the wrong style (too informal). Paragraph (b) is appropriate in style, but it does not introduce the report; it merely discusses other aspects of the same problem. Paragraph (c) is to be preferred because it introduces the main points of the report, and these are expressed in a style appropriate to the report as a whole.

4.6

The second paragraph is to be preferred. The first paragraph is difficult to follow because the various reasons seem to have been grouped together (**in the first place** ...; **secondly** ..., and so on) but the groups themselves are not homogeneous. In other words, there is no reason behind these groupings. In the second paragraph, on the other hand, the groups are: health, convenience, cost and psychological aspect. Learners should apply similar reasoning to group the points they make about cycling.

4.7

One possible version of the report is:

Dear Sirs,

This is my first report to the Association; it is the result
of my experience during the first month of having a guide dog.
On the whole, I must say that my dog, Sheila, has changed my
life for the better; she has made me happier and more independent.

The most important point, perhaps, is my new independence.
Previously I had to rely on other people to take me everywhere.
Now I not only go to work on my own, but I can easily go to
the shops, or to the cinema or a concert, without troubling
anyone else. I feel confident in going out like this because
Sheila makes me feel quite safe in traffic.

More independence was what I had expected from my guide dog,
but one thing I didn't expect was that Sheila would lead me
to make new friends. When I'm out with her, people often
start talking to me, especially when I take her to the park.
In this way I've got to know several people that I'd never
talked to before. I do not feel alone at home, either, because
Sheila is always there to keep me company. Incidentally, you
pointed out to me that Sheila would need plenty of exercise,
but this also means that I myself get more exercise than I
used to, and I feel a lot better for it.

There are only two points that worry me, and I wonder if you
could help me with them. One is the question of Sheila's food.
How can I make sure that I'm giving her enough? The other
problem is that when she's out walking, Sheila doesn't mind
getting her legs wet, so she walks straight through puddles
and so on. This means, of course, that I get my feet wet, too.
Is there anything I can do about this?

Apart from these two minor problems, I am, as I said, very
happy with Sheila, and I am sure that we will continue to get on
very well together.

4.8

One possible version of the journey is:

The first two or three miles from Lake Zurich
were relatively easy, but after passing through
the Forest of Liechtenstein, we came up against
our first mountain pass. At this stage we had
to change gear frequently, and as a result our
driving became slower. As we carried on through
this mountainous section, we had to stop
frequently to make sure the engine/wasn't over-
heating.

The third part of our drive towards Como was
varied. As we drove across the plateau of Thusis,
the road was sometimes flat and straight, but
sometimes mountainous with bends. Although the
road was straighter on average than the Chur road,
we couldn't drive much faster because it was
never straight for long, and we had to keep
changing gear, which reduces speed considerably.

During the last stage we had to go through an
even higher mountain pass, and on several
occasions the car did in fact overheat and we
had to stop and let it cool down. However, with
a great deal of patience we finally reached
Chiavenna six hours after leaving Zurich.

---

5 BROCHURES AND GUIDES

5.1

Sentences 2, 4, 6 and 8 contain an extra word which expresses the relation
between the two clauses. This linking word makes the sentences easier to
follow, and it allows the use of the comma. Without a linking word, the
clauses must be separated by heavier punctuation.

9   You can visit the famous buildings by bus, and you can also take a
horse-drawn cab. (Or **but** or **or** instead of **and**.) Another possibility is
to replace the comma by a full stop or a semicolon.

10   The concerts usually start when the sun has gone down, and they last
for about two and a half to three hours. (Another possibility is to
replace the comma by a full stop or a semicolon.)

11   We will spend part of the day by the sea, so bring a swimsuit.

12 Our guides are all experienced; most of them speak several languages,
and in any case all of them speak English.
Our guides are all experienced, and most of them speak several languages; in any case all of them speak English.
13 The bus leaves at 11 o'clock, and we have lunch in a delightful little
restaurant on top of the cliffs. Then we visit the caves in the afternoon,
and finally we have a guided tour of the old town. (Another alternative,
though not so elegant, would be to change all the commas to semicolons.)
14 Munich is sometimes called the village with a million people; it is the
capital of Bavaria, and it has wonderful art museums and churches.

5.2

j f a g k e b h d i c

5.3

1 (d)   2 (b)   3 (a)   4 (c)   5 (b)   6 (a)   7 (a)
8 (b)   9 (c)   10 (a)   11 namely   12 In other words
13 for instance, for example   14 i.e., that is, that is to say
15 or rather
Possible completions of 16–24 are:
16 those appliances that are normally used in the home.
17 fridges, washing machines, etc.
18 the best time for a visit is June or September.
19 Russia and America.
20 everything except shellfish.
21 the albatross
22 mercury.
23 skiing and skating
24 schools where students learn quickly

5.4

It is clear that each paragraph should contain ideas related to one aspect of
a topic, and that each paragraph should deal with a different aspect of the
topic. In practice, though, there is no one watertight way to carry this out;
in particular, certain styles of writing, e.g. popular journalism, favour short
paragraphs, while other styles might favour fewer divisions. For the piece in
question, here are the most likely possibilities:

London has ... in London for you.

Most visitors ... the shop for you.
(This paragraph could well form one with the previous one.)

You will probably ... along the Thames.

Then there are the arts ... the Tate Gallery.
(This paragraph could join the previous one.)

In the evening ... every day.

Turning to the question ... cheap meals.
(This paragraph could join the previous one.)

This brief survey ... tired of life.'

5.6

The second text is to be preferred; the first is unnecessarily filled out with a great deal of information about the idiosyncratic views and tastes of the author. One improved version of this is:

The famous Roman city of Chester is twenty miles south-east of Liverpool, and can be easily reached by train or bus. The town, although small, is well worth a visit, and visitors should pay particular attention to the following places of interest. First, there are the Roman baths, and the remains of the Roman walls, both situated in beautiful surroundings at the side of the River Dee. Second, and close by, is the famous Tudor shopping centre called 'The Rows'. You can spend hours walking along these raised wooden passageways, peering into the numerous shops and old-fashioned pubs. Another famous feature of Chester is its Zoo, which is one of the largest and most modern in Europe; there is a direct bus from the city centre. If you are lucky enough to visit Chester in the summer, then you should visit Chester races, which are a truly magnificent spectacle. But whatever the season, this charming city will provide the tourist with a varied and interesting stay.

6 ARTICLES

6.1

We use a colon typically to indicate that what follows will make explicit what has been suggested or implied in a general way in the first half of the sentence. In 1 and 2, the second half in fact lists what is stated generally in the first half.

One main use of the semicolon (5–8) is to separate two clauses that are balanced both in structure and subject matter; the two clauses usually show some degree of contrast.

Another use of the semicolon is to clarify sentences which would be ambiguous if only commas were used. In 9 there is a list of four separate items of equipment; the only function of the comma here is to separate the items. In 10 there is only one item of equipment, namely a small motor, and we are told that this was fitted with a transformer, wire and a switch. Here the comma has two roles: the first serves to indicate the beginning of a non-defining relative clause; the second separates items in a list. If, on the other hand, the wire and the switch are separate items, then we can only indicate

this clearly with the punctuation of 11. Here there are three items, and we are told that the motor was fitted with a transformer.
12 The reason was obvious: they could not afford the fare.
13 The summer is short and intense; the winter is long but mild.
14 There were two obvious suspects: Bryanston and Waites.
15 Each team was allowed the following: 10 kilos of food, including fruit; water; salt; and ample petrol.
16 Each team was allowed the following: 10 kilos of food, including fruit, water and salt; and ample petrol.
17 The garden was decorated with coloured lamps; the house itself was adorned with paper chains.
18 The estate consisted of a large forest complete with hunting lodge; several meadows; a lake; and about 30 acres of arable land.
19 Yorkshire, which was the largest county, was split into three new administrative areas; Rutland, which was the smallest county, was absorbed into the neighbouring area.
20 They made two important decisions: the oldest houses would be pulled down; the more recent ones would be repaired.

6.2

e   k   d   g   a   i   c   h   f   j   b

6.3

1 (b)   2 (c)   3 (c)   4 (c)   5 (a)   6 (a)   7 (b)
8 (b)   9 (c)   10 (b)   11 (a)   12 (a)   13 (c)
14 (b)

6.4

Preferred first paragraph: (b). This tells the reader that Mrs Gordon has been acting in the public interest against offenders; it is the best introductory paragraph because it relates the heroine to the story, and it does so in a way that attracts the reader's attention.
   Paragraph (a) explains what the law is, but it does not introduce either Mrs Gordon or the article in general.
   Paragraph (c) mentions Mrs Gordon, but it is vague, badly written and disconnected.
Preferred last paragraph: (c). This paragraph nicely summarises Mrs Gordon's attitude to the whole business, and it uses her own words to round off the article.
   Paragraph (a) uses a chatty style that is unlike the rest of the article; it also throws in a lot of irrelevant personal opinions.
   Paragraph (b), in spite of beginning 'In summary', does not summarise the article; it introduces statistics which do not round off the piece.

6.6

One possible version of the article is:

Perlbury sailor attempts Atlantic Record

Georgina Nugent reports on the amazing courage of local boy Derek Towers, who is a lone yachtsman and member of the Perlbury Sailing Club.

Derek has just returned home in time for Christmas after a heroic thirty-day ordeal in which he attempted to beat the record for sailing across the Atlantic single handed—and in a thirty-foot boat! Unfortunately, he didn't quite succeed because he ran into some very unpleasant weather. I asked Derek how he had felt during the trip, and he explained that a lone sailor experiences all sorts of different feelings, but in the end he gets used to anything. In any case there was so much work to do on board that he didn't have time to worry.

Derek also explained that he didn't stay awake for the whole thirty days. His boat is equipped with automatic steering rather like a wind vane, and as long as the wind doesn't change direction, everything will be all right. I asked him what happened if the wind changed and whether there wasn't a danger of collision when he was asleep. He assured me that he would wake up instinctively if there was any change in the movement of the boat, and that the chances of a crash are very slight.

When I asked Derek when he was going to make another attempt, his immediate reaction was: 'Never again!' But then he laughed and said that I should ask him again after Christmas.

I think that the whole of Perlbury should feel proud of Derek's courage and determination. I hope that everybody will join me when I say to him: 'Congratulations, and better luck next time!'

6.7

One possible version of the article is:

Progress of Killer Germ Epidemic in Juiyo Fulikim

IN DECEMBER 1977 and January 1978, the death rate in Juiyo Fulikim was steady at around 2 or 3 a month. At the beginning of February, however, a small group of migrant workers, who had been working in an infected area, returned to the district. There was an immediate sharp increase in the number of deaths, and local doctors at once suspected the killer germ.

That year there was a very dry spring, which led to a lack of safe drinking water, and this resulted in an even sharper rise in the death rate. Fortunately, in April the government managed to introduce quarantine measures, which stopped the rapid spread of the epidemic. The increase in the death rate was halted and, in fact, the rate started to decline.

At the end of May the World Health Organisation sent a limited supply of medicine to combat the effects of the germ, and there was an immediate sharp fall in the rate. Unfortunately, after only a few days, and for reasons that are still not clear, the medicine began to lose its effect and, though the rate continued to fall, this was not as marked as before.

This gradual decline lasted until mid-July, when the rate once again turned upwards. This new development was, according to the doctors working on the case, due to a virulent strain of the germ, which resisted the medicine supplied by the WHO.

At the end of August, the team of doctors finally managed to produce a vaccine, which was immediately administered to the whole population of Juiyo Fulikim. This produced a dramatic drop in the death-rate, and smiles returned to the faces of the local people. From mid-September to the end of the year, the death rate fell gradually to the pre-epidemic level, where it has remained up to the present.

7 INSTRUCTIONS

7.1

Put a cupful of hot water and a stock cube in a deep casserole, and put this on a low heat. Sprinkle salt over the pieces of liver, and dip each piece in flour. Fry the liver briefly in hot oil so as to seal in the juices. When each piece is brown, transfer it to the casserole. Now chop the carrots, onions and garlic, and put them in the casserole. Remove the skins from the tomatoes, and add the juice to the other ingredients. Season to taste, but leave the pepper to be added towards the end. Simmer on a low heat for about 1½ hours. When the stew is ready to serve, grind the black pepper over it.

7.2

f   i   a   j   b   l   e   k   g   d   h   c

7.3

In a way both (a) and (b) are correct; however, (a) follows the so-called rules for reported speech slavishly, while (b) provides a more concise report. It is the reporting word *ask* (in the sense of 'request') which makes this possible, since reporting words express the main feeling of what was said, allowing the report itself to be kept short. In real life, therefore, (b) will virtually always be preferred to (a).

1 Yvonne encouraged Tony to make a cake.
2 The headmaster ordered Jones to pick up the papers (at once).
3 Fred begged Jane to help him.
4 Miss Pritchard allowed the boys to go home.
5 Mr Bream warned the children not to go too near the edge.
   Mr Bream warned the children about going too near the edge.

7.5

The first letter is to be preferred. A better version of the second letter is:

> Flat 5,
> St. Martins Court,
> London.   N8
>
> 3 July 1982
>
> Dear Mr and Mrs Levy,
>
> Both my wife and I are happy to know that you will definitely be coming to
> stay in our house next month. As requested, here are the instructions for
> what to do when you arrive.
>
> First of all, you can pick up the keys from the IHES office in Brandt Street.
> There are three keys: one large one for the main door of the building, and the
> two smaller ones for the door of the flat. Please lock both doors every time
> you go out. Arnold Gold on the first floor will have the keys to the garage.
>
> When you enter the flat you will find everything turned off. The main switch
> for the electricity is in the cupboard on your right as you come in through
> the front door. The main water tap is under the sink in the kitchen. The
> central heating, in case you need it, is controlled from a switch on the wall
> by the kitchen door. The main switch for the central heating is under the
> stairs.
>
> You'll be able to find clean sheets and towels in the tall cupboard in the
> middle of the main passage. Please help yourself to anything at all you might
> need.
>
> We would be very grateful if you would be so kind as to look after the plants
> while we are away. Please water them at least once a day, preferably in the
> morning — and don't forget the ones on the balcony!
>
> When you leave, please turn everything off, and leave the keys with the porter.
>
> I think that's everything. If you should have any trouble (the washing
> machine has its off days, and the garage door's a bit temperamental) Arnold
> Gold is a very helpful man who understands these things. I'm sure everything
> will be all right.
>
> I hope you enjoy your stay,
>
> yours,
>
> *Peter Rogers*
>
> Peter Rogers.

7.6

One possible version of the instructions is:

1 First make sure that the machine is plugged into the mains (220 volts),
   and that the water tap is open.
2 Set the temperature control to 30°.
3 In order to protect these delicate woollen clothes, press in Buttons A and
   B.
4 Fill the powder drawer with soap flakes, not detergent, and shut the
   drawer tight.
5 Do not use any bleach.
6 Set the programme selector to 'not very dirty clothes', and pull it out to
   start the machine working.

7 When the programme selector reaches 'end', push in this button to switch the machine off.
8 Take out the garments, and lay them flat in a warm place to dry. Do not iron them.

8 WRITING A STORY

8.1

11 'Did John come?' asked Michael.
12 'We are,' she insisted, 'the oldest family around here.'
13 'Leave me alone!' he roared.
14 Then Mrs Smith asked, 'Where on earth were they?'
15 'They've gone,' replied the countess, 'and they won't be coming back.'
16 'It's very nice,' she said quietly. 'Where did you buy it?'
17 'I'd simply like to know,' my neighbour whispered, 'where the woman lives.'
18 'Yes, I do,' I said in a loud voice.
19 'Well,' he mumbled, 'I don't really know what to say.'
20 The farmer shouted, 'What the hell are you doing in there?'
21 'I might come with you,' she said. 'Where exactly are you going?'
22 'They're all out,' replied the maid, 'and I've no idea when they'll be back.'
23 'What?' my mother shouted. 'Don't you dare say that again!'
24 The old man whispered, 'I can't really go very fast. Where can I sit down?'
25 'No,' she said, 'I'm afraid I can't do anything for you.'
26 'What's your telephone number?' Susan asked with a smile.

8.2

e   b   j   c   g   a   k   i   d   h   f

8.3

1 (a) or (c)   2 (a) or (b)   3 (a)   4 (a) or (b) though *moreover* is perhaps too formal in this text   5 (d)   6 (b)   7 (b) or (c)
8 (a)   9 (c)   10 (b) or (c)   11 (a)   12 (a) or (c)
13 (a)   14 (b)   15 (a)   16 (a) or (c)   17 (a) or (b)
18 (b)   19 (a) or (b)   20 (c)

8.4

In a way both (a) and (b) are correct; however, (b) follows the so-called rules for reported speech slavishly, while (a) provides a more concise report. It is the reporting word *threaten* that makes this possible, since reporting words express the main feeling of what was said, allowing the report itself to be kept short. In real life, therefore, (a) will virtually always be preferred to (b).

1 Fanny complained that the company (had) treated her unfairly.
 Fanny complained about the company's unfair treatment (of her).
2 Anne remembered that it was her mother's birthday.
3 Kate reminded me (her, etc.) how to get to the park.
4 Mr Jackson suspected the neighbours of telling the police.
 Mr Jackson suspected the neighbours of having told the police.
5 Nellie offered to baby-sit for us (them, etc.).
 Nellie offered to take care of the children so that we (they, etc.) could go out.

8.5

Preferred first sentence: (c).
Preferred last sentence: (f).

8.6

The second paragraph is to be preferred; the sentences are well joined together, and this makes it easier for the reader to follow. The first paragraph, on the other hand, consists of many short, badly connected sentences.

8.7

One possible version of the letter is:

```
Dear Mum and Dad

I hope you are both well and enjoying life in Tokyo. Unfortunately,
I've got some very bad news for you: we've been burgled! I know you
will think that it's my fault, but I can assure you that I always
take the usual precautions. Anyway, I'm very sorry, and I'd better
just tell you what happened.

Last Thursday I came back from my Italian class at about 10.30, and
I found the whole house in absolute chaos. Apparently the burglars
had forced their way in through the kitchen door, and then they had
been right through the house, turning everything upside down. It was
a terrible mess, but now I've more or less got things back in their
places.

As to what is missing, they took the radio, the TV, the stereo, all
your records, and also some of the paintings. I'm afraid I can't say
exactly what they've taken out of the drawers because I don't really
know what was in all of them. This is a problem because the police
insist on having a list of the missing items before they start their
investigations. (By the way, they don't seem very optimistic about
recovering anything.) I know it would mean a great inconvenience and
expense, but if one of you could come back early, it would be a great
help. I'm very sorry for the trouble but I can't help it.

Apart from the burglary, everything else is more or less all right.

        Hope to hear from you soon.
```

9 BUSINESS LETTERS AND MEMOS

9.1

Dear Sirs,

My recent order, which arrived safely, contained two items: one Red Pyjama and one White Stripe Pyjama.

Our daughter is four and a half months old, weighs 7 kilos(,) and is 61 centimetres long. In other words, she is a fairly average size for her age. Given this, we were confident that the right size of pyjama for her would be the 70 cm, which you claim will last until baby is some nine months old. To our great disappointment(,) the Red is a tight fit now, while the White Stripe is a comfortable fit now, and may last, say, one or two months.

Misleading labelling and predictions are unfortunate in any circumstances, but doubly so when the customer lives abroad. Apart from the trouble and cost of returning the things, the fact is that our daughter needs the garments that we ordered now, and we can thus hardly afford any delay. Could you please let me know whether it is your normal policy to overestimate the age and size for which a particular garment is suitable? If this is so, then we can simply take it into account when we make orders in the future.

I would like to point out that we are in general happy with your goods. It is only the question of size which we find extremely irritating.

Yours faithfully,

Robin Purdue

Robin Purdue

9.2

f   k   c   g   b   i   a   h   e   j   d

9.3

1 (b)	2 (a)	3 (b)	4 (a)	5 (b)	6 (a)	7 (b)
8 (c)	9 (c)	10 (a)	11 (b)	12 (c)	13 (c)	
14 (a)	15 (a)	16 (a)	17 (b)	18 (b)		

9.4

In a way both (a) and (b) are correct; however, (b) follows the so-called rules for reported speech slavishly, while (a) provides a more concise report. It is the reporting words *admit* and *promise* that make this possible, since reporting words express the main feeling of what was said, allowing the report itself to be kept short. In real life, therefore, (a) will virtually always be preferred to (b).

1 The chief engineer assumed that they had read the report, and had invited comments from their designer.
2 The mayor's assistant refused to allow Mr Winterbottom to see the mayor, and insisted that he (should) leave the office.
3 The works manager insisted that there was something wrong with the machine, and warned them not to use it before it had been serviced.
4 The manageress promised not to tell anyone and invited Mr Ridgeway to give her his comments.
5 The accountant denied that we had overcharged them, and suggested that they should compare our prices with those of our competitors.
6 The director greeted Thomson, and asked him if there was any post.

9.5

Preferred first paragraph: B.
Suggested first paragraph:
We thank you for your letter of 28 September 1980. We are pleased that you are prepared to supply us with the new XL lathes, and we are satisfied with the basic cost of these. However, there are two problems that we would like to raise with you.

Preferred last paragraph: B.
Suggested last paragraph:
I would therefore like to make two suggestions to improve our stand at future exhibitions. First, I recommend that we increase the area of our stand to, say, 60 square metres so as to give us sufficient room to display more of our books for teaching English to foreigners. Second, I feel it is essential that the staff should include at least one expert in this new field who can then deal on the spot with enquiries from specialists. I would be pleased to hear your views on these two proposals.

9.6

The first letter is to be preferred because the second, although it contains all
the necessary information, is disorganised, and has not been separated into
paragraphs dealing with different aspects. One improved version of the
second letter is:

Dear Sirs,

I would like to apply for the post of
Works Manager, which was advertised in
The Guardian of 22 October 1982. I feel
that my qualifications and experience are
ideally suited for the position.

I was born in 1945, and I went to school from
1950 to 1965. In 1964 I took the General
Certificate of Education, and I got good
grades in Maths, Physics and Chemistry.
After leaving school, I attended Bristol
Technical College, where I first studied
Fibre Technology and Colour Chemistry; later
I studied the other subjects related to tex-
tile manufacture, and in 1968 I obtained
the Diploma in Textiles.

After completing my studies, I joined the
Topp Clothing Company, where I worked until
1973. In that year I moved to Prior
Productions, who were pleased with my work,
and as a result in 1978 I was promoted to
Assistant Works Manager there.

I enjoy my work, and I am prepared to work
hard; moreover, I am sure that Prior
Productions would give me an excellent
reference. I therefore feel that my
application deserves your serious
consideration.

I look forward to hearing from you.

Yours faithfully,

Colin Whitfield

Colin Whitfield.

9.7

Hornby & Sons
Special Steels

Memo from: G. Bennett   To: A. J. George

Thank you for your suggestions regarding the
changing facilities provided for your staff.
The management is, of course, aware of the
problem, but unfortunately your suggestions
cannot be accepted for the following reasons:

1. The old canteen site is not available for
   building, as it will shortly be converted
   into extra warehouse space.

2. Your proposal to use existing warehouse
   space would mean unacceptable pressure
   on the available space, which you must
   know is already inadequate.

3. The expense involved in both your
   suggestions is very high, and the company
   is not in a position to invest large sums
   of money at this time.

4. I think you will find that very few of
   the men employed in your section actually
   need a shower at the end of the day, and
   these could easily share the Gate-House
   facilities, which are nearby.

5. As all the women employed in the warehouse are engaged in purely clerical
   work, I cannot see that the section of
   the Factories Act that you quote is in
   fact applicable in this case.

However, the provision of separate toilets for
men and women would be a great improvement.
I have therefore asked the building department
to look into this. I have also asked them to
repair the existing facilities in the warehouse area.